YOU AND YOUR BRAIN

A NEUROSCIENTIST EXPLAINS THE NERVOUS SYSTEM TO HIS GRANDSON

Dale Purves

You and Your Brain

Book Baby (Amazon)

ISBN 978-1-09831-292-3

Back cover photo by Woody Burns

Hi Will-

Since you are nearly ten and a smart guy interested in science, I thought I would put down for you in a short book how brains work. Neuroscience—the name of the field that studies brains and the rest of the rest of the nervous system—is not all that complicated and a lot more interesting right now than most science. Even though I have been at it for fifty years now I have never been bored. Often frustrated by the difficulty of the questions that need to be answered and my stupidity in trying to solve them—but never bored. Anyway, after so many years I know a lot about the subject—or at least I think I do—and want to pass along some facts and explanations to you and kids about your age who are up for it.

Most things are explained as I go along in the short chapters that follow, but some words will probably be unfamiliar. Thus I've added a mini-dictionary at the end that defines of the trickier terms. I have also put the key words you need to pay attention to in italics and added some pictures (scientists call them "Figures") to make the story easier to follow.

So here we go!

Love,

Dale

Chapter 1

Some Basic Info

It's always a good idea to start a scientific chat with some important definitions and descriptions, so let's begin by defining the human brain and the rest of the nervous system in the body and describing their major   features. Actually, most living things in the world get along fine without brains and nervous systems, which raises some important questions; but let's come back to that later. For starters, the brain is defined as the part of the nervous system that sits inside your skull, which you can see as the tan thing in Figure 1.

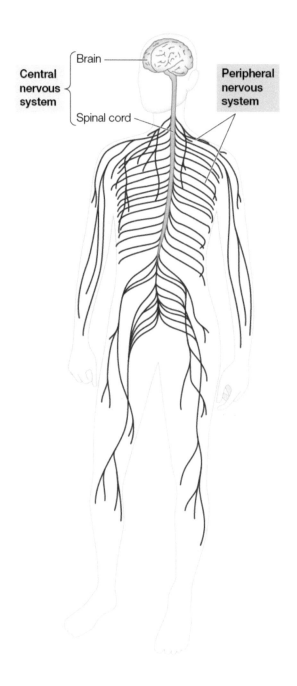

Figure 1. The brain and the rest of the nervous system.

Figure 2 shows that the brain consists of two halves called the *cerebral hemispheres*, each of which includes four large areas called *lobes.* The names of the areas come from the bones of the skull that lie over them, and each of the lobes is focused on doing different things (although they also communicate with each other big time). The *frontal lobe* is generally thought to be where most our personality comes from as well as our sense of right and wrong; the *parietal lobe* helps guide our attention to meaningful things that are going on in the world; the *temporal lobe* is important in recognizing specific objects like tables and chairs; and the *occipital lobe* makes it possible to see. Of course, it's not that simple. Each one of these lobes is carrying out other jobs as well, some of which I'll talk about later.

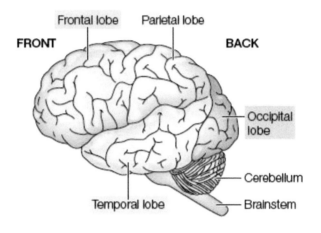

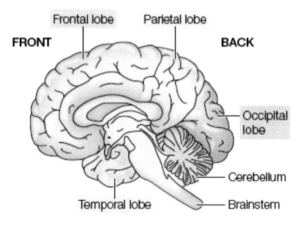

Figure 2. The cerebral hemispheres and their four lobes. The top picture shows the left cerebral hemisphere as seen from the side. The bottom picture shows the right cerebral hemisphere seen from the middle of the brain with the left hemisphere removed. The *cerebellum* is a more or less separate part of the brain that helps us carry difficult acts—for example, juggling your soccer ball on one foot— that require a lot of coordination. The cerebellum is not very well understood, but then many other parts of the brain aren't well

8

understood either. The *brainstem* connects the cerebral hemispheres and the cerebellum to the *spinal cord* and the rest of the nervous system, as you can see in Figure 1. When we talk about the two hemispheres together, they are called the *cerebrum*.

Some of the surface bumps and dips that you see on the brain surface in Figure 2 help set the four lobes apart in each hemisphere. But when you are looking at a real brain, specific bumps and valleys are actually hard to find because they vary a lot from one person's brain to another person's brain. That's a big part of what makes each of us different. But you need some landmarks to talk about brains, and these bumps and dips have been used for a long time as rough guides to the four lobes of the hemispheres and what each of the different regions does.

Oh, and take note of the *cerebellum* tucked under the back of the brain. The cerebral hemispheres and the cerebellum are attached to the spinal cord by the *brainstem*, and these four structures—the *cerebral hemispheres, the brainstem, the cerebellum and spinal cord*—make up the *central nervous system*.

Chapter 2

How Brains and Bodies are Connected

Figure 3 shows the connection between the brain and spinal cord. The spinal cord runs inside the bony spinal column that you can feel down the middle of your back when you put your finders there. What you feel are the spines coming off each of the 24 bones called vertebrae that encase the spinal cord, ending with the tailbone, which you can also feel between the cheeks of your butt. All these bones protect the spinal cord and the nerves coming off it from getting hurt. You have probably heard of people who had their spinal cord damaged in a car crash, in rough sports like American football or in banging dive into a pool that was too shallow. If the damage is bad, the victim is unable to feel anything—or move any muscles—below the injury to the spine and spinal cord. The loss of feeling and mobility is usually permanent because the spinal cord can't repair itself. As a result, the information going up and down the cord can't get through the damaged region.

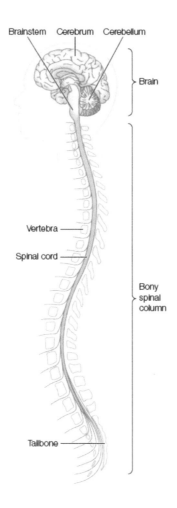

Figure 3. The brain, spinal cord and bony spinal column. Altogether, the cerebral hemispheres, the cerebellum, brainstem and the spinal cord make up the *central nervous system* as shown in Figure 1.

The *peripheral nerves* shown in Figure 1 come out from the brainstem and spinal cord as thick bundles of *nerve fibers* that carry information to and from the rest of the body. The most obvious targets are the *skeletal muscles*—about 700 in all—that let us to move our arms, legs and other body parts where muscles move the bones that make up the skeleton. Other nerves come off the brainstem to control movements that do specific things—like the tongue, the swallowing muscles in the throat and the muscles that move the eyes. They are not shown in Figure 1 but are just as important as the muscles that move to the skeletal bones.

Of course, the information coming *to* the brain and the rest of the central nervous system is at least as important as the information going out from the spinal cord and brainstem. We wouldn't stay alive for long without this the information coming from the eyes, ear, nose and a lot of other less obvious *sense organs*. An example is children (fortunately, very few) born with a nervous system defect that prevents them from feel pain. As a result they suffer cuts, bruises, broken bones and other injuries that the sensation of pain in normal nervous system would have helped them avoid.

Other targets of peripheral nerves in the body are called *organs* if they are big and separate like the heart, lungs, stomach and others shown in Figure 4. The peripheral nerves also carry information to lots of muscles that are different from the skeletal muscles. These are called *smooth muscles* let our organs act without our having to think about it. For example, thank about how your digestive system works. The muscles in the walls of your stomach and intestines move food along and cause the gurgles you sometimes hear. The gurgles come from bubbles of gas mixed in with the food and end up as farts. Other smooth muscles in the walls of your blood vessels. When you are frightened or cold, these muscles contract and make you turn pale. When they relax, the blood vessels in your skin enlarge and make your skin feel hot if you blush have done something you think is wrong, dumb or otherwise embarrassing. A third type of muscle is the heart—and there is only one of these. *Heart muscle* is special because unlike other muscles the heart has to work 24/7 to pump the blood around the body. The different things that skeletal muscles, smooth muscles and the heart muscle make possible—most of which we are not aware of—is obviously a big deal.

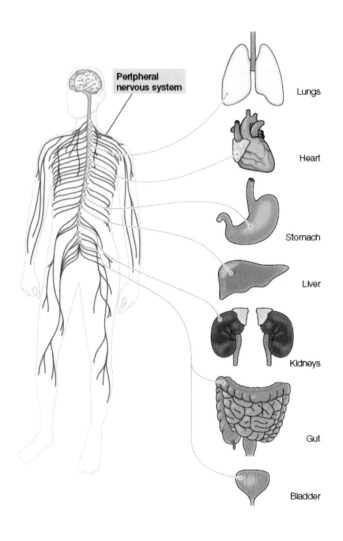

Figure 4. **Contraction and relaxation of body organs by smooth muscles and hear muscle.** Control of the smooth muscles in organs such as the heart, lungs, intestines, kidneys and bladder is driven by small collections of nerve cells called *ganglia* (the little

14

green circles) that are outside the central nervous system near the spinal cord or often near the organs themselves. The nerve fibers coming from the nerve cells in these ganglia run in the peripheral nerves as well. The stuff shown in green is called the *autonomic nervous system* and it has two parts: an activating or excitatory part made up the green circles next to the spinal cord and a relaxing or inhibitory part made up of the green circles near the organs. The autonomic nervous system thus provides a sort of on-off control of the body's organs that goes on automatically without our having to think.

Chapter 3

How Cells Work

So far we've been looking only at what can be seen with our own eyes. So let's dig a little deeper into the cells of the nervous system and see how they work. I'm sure you know something about *cells* and that much of the human body is made up of these tiny units. You also know that cells come in many types including blood cells, muscle cells, skin cells, fat cells—the list goes on and on. Keep in mind, too, that we are made up of other things. For instance, our teeth and most of our bones are just mineral stuff. And if you were to squash us in a giant garlic press, you'd find that about 70 percent of our body weight overall is actually just water.

Most cells are so tiny you need a microscope to see them. A typical size is 100 *micrometers* in diameter, a micrometer being one-thousandth of a *millimeter,* which is one-tenth of a *centimeter*, which is one-hundredth of a *meter.* Scientists use the *metric system* and not the system of inches, feet and yards that most Americans use, so anyone who enters the world of science has to get used to metric measurements (I added a Conversion Table at the end). All cells have a thin skin called a *membrane* surrounding them. The membrane is about the thickness of the outside of a soap bubble, and is actually pretty much like a soap bubble, seeing as how it's made up of oily stuff that tends to form a sphere. But some cells are much larger. For instance, when you pull apart a chicken tender, it usually separates into bundles of fibers that you can see. These are groups of muscle cells that reach across the whole breast muscle in a chicken, a distance that may be 5 to 10 centimeters.

And although nerve cells like other cells have tiny more or less spherical cell bodies that are roughly 10 to 100 micrometers (abbreviated as *microns*), most of them have long narrow branches coming off their cell bodies, as you can see in Figure 5. The branches coming off cell bodies receive and pass on information from or to other nerve cells or to targets like skeletal muscles or the smooth muscles in organs. Once you take their branches into account, nerve cells are all over the map in terms of size.

17

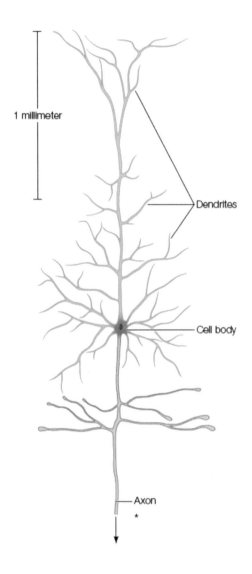

1 millimeter

Dendrites

Cell body

Axon

*

Figure 5. A typical nerve cell in the brain and its branches. The *cell body* is the red thing in the middle with branches coming off it. One branch, the tan-colored one called the *axon*, can travel a long way. The nerve cells going from the spinal cord to the muscles in your foot, for example, are tens of centimeters long and will get even

18

longer as you continue growing taller. Same deal for axons going in the other direction, for example from pain sensors in your foot to your spinal cord if you step on a tack. Other branches (the bluish ones) are called *dendrites;* they don't go very far. Their function to receive information from other nerve cells, as described in Chapter 6.

You need to know much more about how information is transferred by these branches, but let's leave that aside for a while and talk more about cells in general. All cells—a typical cell is diagrammed in Figure 6—contain inside their membranes even tinier structures called *organelles*. These little guys allow cells to work in a variety of different ways. The main organelle in any cell is the *nucleus*, which contains the cell's *genetic code* stored in a coiled-up DNA *molecule*, as you have probably heard. The genetic code in the cell's DNA tells the cell what type it is and what functions to carry out (remember, there are many kinds of cells).

Another important organelle in cells is the *mitochondrion.* There are lots of mitochondria in almost every type of cell, and each of them can be thought of as a miniature factory where chemical energy is made. A cell needs that energy to do the particular job it's been programmed to carry out. A third kind of organelle is fibers called *microtubules*. These act like a skeleton and keep the cell from collapsing into a pancake.

Cells also contain thousands of different kinds of *protein molecules* that carry out chemical reactions in cells. For example, red blood cells are filled with protein molecules called *hemoglobin*, which carry oxygen to all the other cells in the body and picks up the carbon dioxide waste they produce that we eventually breathe out from the lungs (red blood cells don't have a nucleus so they can pack in more hemoglobin and do their job a little better). By the way, the nervous system is *not* made up of just nerve cells. There are many other cells in the nervous system, called *neuroglia*, that keep the nerve cells happy and healthy in different ways. In fact, the brain and the rest of the nervous system contain a lot more of these "supporting" cells than nerve cells. Because the nervous system has to have a steady supply of oxygen and nutrients, it is also full of blood vessels and the cells that make them up, such the smooth muscle cells in their walls.

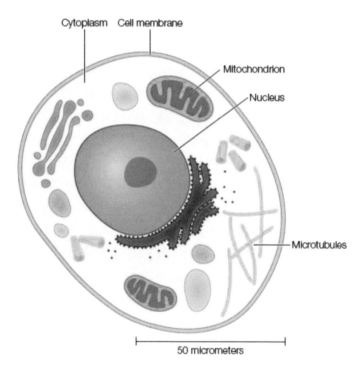

Cytoplasm   Cell membrane
Mitochondrion
Nucleus
Microtubules
50 micrometers

Figure 6. A typical cell and its organs. Unlike nerve cells, other cells don't have axons and dendrite. But the contents of the cell body of a nerve cell (see Figure 5) are similar to the contents all cells. The fluid that fills the cells is called the *cytoplasm*, and all the little things floating around in it are *organelles* that do different jobs to keep the cell working normally.

Although these general facts about cells can help you understand what nerve cells do and how they differ from other cells, they don't give you a very clear idea of how nerve cells make the brain and nervous system special. The facts I've laid out so far say nothing about the inside of the brain or, more importantly, what the brain *does* and how nerve cells make what it does happen.

Chapter 4

Looking Inside the Brain

Let's begin with what the brain looks like on the inside. When someone dies, doctors may ask the family if it would be OK to remove the brain—and other organs—to determine what caused the death and whether and the treatment the patient received were on the money or not. That process is called an autopsy. Actually, fewer autopsies are performed these days because so many tests can be done while the patients are still alive. But looking at the brain after a person dies is still pretty common since even fancy brain-imaging methods carried out in patients can't tell all that much about nervous-system diseases.

What, then, does the doctor look for? When the brain is removed from a dead person after sawing away the top of the skull, it is a tannish, wrinkled blob weighing about 1.5 kilos (1500 grams or about 3 pounds) that has more or less the consistency of Jell-O. The surface appearance is pretty much as shown in the diagrams in Figure 2, minus the added colors. The doctor first examines how the brain looks from the outside. Is it shrunken, as it often is in older people? Is there any sign of a cancer? Could a stroke have killed a part of the brain? Are there any other abnormal features? The brain is then cut into a dozen or so slices (about the thickness of a piece of bread) to check for any anything odd that wasn't obvious from the surface (Figure 7).

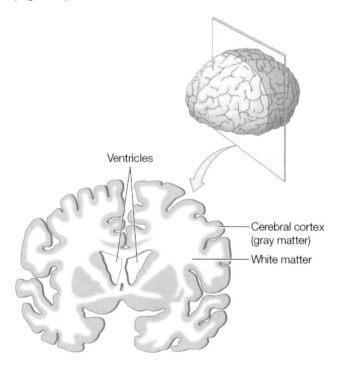

Ventricles

Cerebral cortex (gray matter)

White matter

Figure 7. A slice cut from the middle of the brain. Notice that some parts of the brain on the inside are grayish tan, like the color of the surface, while other parts are whitish. The tan parts (generally referred to as "gray" rather than tan) are where the nerve cell bodies and the dendrite branches are located. The whitish parts are the axons running to other parts of the brain and down to (and up from) the spinal cord. That's why when you think somebody is smart, you say the person "has a lot of gray matter." (Actually, it doesn't really work that way: when Einstein's brain was examined after his death, he turned out to have a less than average amount of gray matter and a rather small brain.) The open spaces in the middle of the slice are called *ventricles*. In a living person, the ventricles are filled with a salty fluid that circulates throughout the brain to help keep its chemistry in balance.

Small chunks (about a cubic centimeter) are often taken out from the bread slices, put in wax. When the wax hardens the chunks are cut into much thinner slices with a knife edge much like a razor blade. The slices—called *microscopic sections*—are then stained with dyes to show up different sorts of cells when the sections are looked at using a *light microscope* (Figure 8). Microscopic sections can also be made by freezing a chunk of tissue removed surgically from a living patient and cutting slices from the frozen piece. These sections let doctors zero in right away on a possibly diseased part. The doctor looking at the frozen section can tell the surgeon whether or not the removed tissue (called a *biopsy*) is something like a cancer that calls for more treatment. The surgeon can then go ahead and take out more of the cancer. But if the sections look harmless, the patient can be sewn up and avoid a second operation later. Interestingly, the brain itself doesn't feel any pain so brain surgery can be carried out while patients are awake.

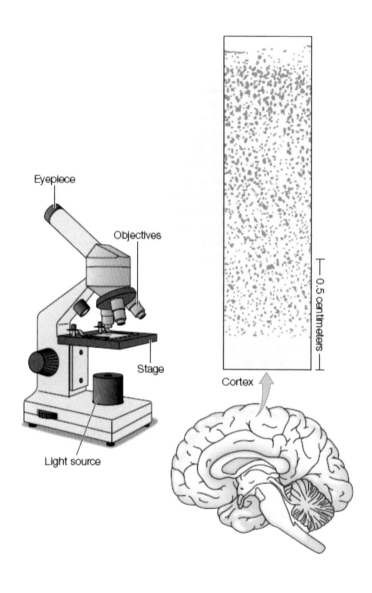

Figure 8. A stained section from the cerebral cortex showing how it would look when viewed in a light microscope (the instrument on the left). The section is placed on the stage and light is shown through it from below. The objectives can be rotated into place to get different levels of magnification. The diagram on the right is what the viewer would see if the section were magnified about 40 times actual size by the lenses in the microscope. The top of the section is the surface of the brain and the bottom is where the white matter begins (see Figure 7). The little dark blobs in the section are nerve cell bodies, as shown in Figure 5. Over the last hundred years or more, this sort of microscopic observation has given doctors and brain scientists a lot to work with as they tried to figure out what different parts of the brain look like and what those parts do.

Sections seen in a light microscope like the one shown in Figure 8 can magnify things in sections up to about a thousand times, revealing a lot of amount of detail. An *electron microscope*, however, can magnify up to tens of thousands of times and so can show a much more detail (Figure 9). The routine use of the electron microscope began in the 1950s, has been used to see many of the smaller organelles diagrammed in Figure 6. Making tissue sections for viewing in an electron microscope is done in much the same way as preparing sections for light microscopy, but using trickier methods. Instead of being put in wax, the tissue is embedded in a plastic much like the epoxy you use to fix things around the house. And instead of a steel blade, a knife edge made out of diamond is used to cut much thinner sections. Finally, the sections have to be stained with a solution of lead to block the electrons. You have to stain the sectionsso that the edges of things show up clearly.

26

Otherwise and you can't see much using either a light or an electron microscopy.

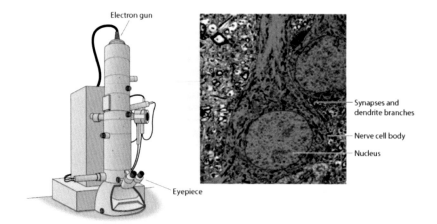

Figure 9. Seeing smaller details in sections viewed with an electron microscope. An electron microscope is much bigger and more complicated than the light microscope (and much more expensive!). Seen through an electron microscope, the tissue section on the right includes two nerve bodies (shaded in purple), which correspond to a couple of the little blobs in Figure 8 at much greater magnification. The nucleus of each cell is the round thing in the middle, and the organelles are all the other stuff you see scattered around within the cell body. The stuff outside the cell bodies is an enormous tangle of nerve cell branches and glial cells.

You might wonder why the magnification using light and the magnification using electrons are so different. Light energy and electron energy both travel as waves. The energy that carries sound also travels as waves, but sound waves are much longer (meters from peak to peak versus tiny fractions of a micrometer for light and electron waves). And the longer the wavelengths the bigger the objects they can get around. Thus when you play hide and seek the tiny light waves can't get around a tree that is hiding you. But the much longer sound waves can, which is why you have to keep quiet if you don't want to be found. For the same reasons electrons waves are blocked much smaller objects in microscopic sections that light waves.

Chapter 5

The Evolution of Brains

Seeing all this detail in the brain has led some scientists to claim the human brain is "the most complex object in the universe." That is not so. For starters, a whale's brain or an elephant's brain is much bigger than our brains, which means they have many more nerve cells and connections between them (Figure 10). This sort of self-important thinking has also caused some philosophers to say that the human brain may never be understood. That idea is also not very smart. The brain is just another organ like those in Figure 4 and, although a lot of puzzles remain today, they will soon enough be understood just like everything else in our bodies.

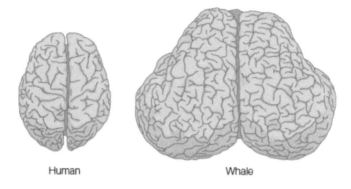

Human   Whale

Figure 10. The size of a human brain compared to the brain of whale (a Fin Whale in this example).

Let's turn to another general question about brains that needs to be answered: how have brains gotten to be the way they are over time? In terms of the time that life has existed on Earth, the answer—as you probably know—is *evolution*, the central idea that explains the structure and function of all living things. The first life on Earth got going nearly four billion years ago as a special kind of *bacteria*. These earliest ancestors of ours are also the ancestors of the bacteria today crawling around today in your gut, on your skin and just about every place else on or near the Earth's surface. How the early bacteria got going from lifeless chemicals is not known, but once they did, the rest is history. Bacteria led to the evolution of more complicated single-cell organisms like the little amoeboid things you can see swimming in a drop of pond water using a light microscope. Then came multi-celled organisms like worms and flies and eventually more complex plants and animals, including us, as diagrammed on the timeline of life on Earth in Figure 11.

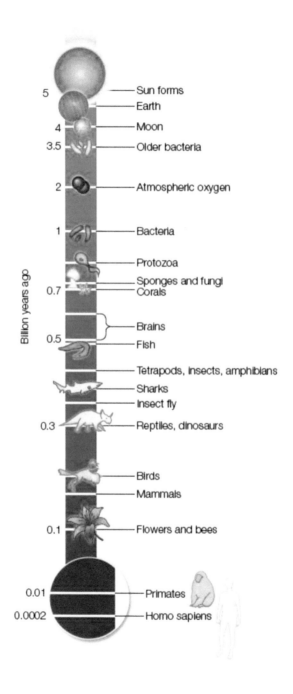

Billion years ago

5	Sun forms
	Earth
4	Moon
3.5	Older bacteria
2	Atmospheric oxygen
1	Bacteria
	Protozoa
0.7	Sponges and fungi / Corals
	Brains
0.5	Fish
	Tetrapods, insects, amphibians
	Sharks
	Insect fly
0.3	Reptiles, dinosaurs
	Birds
	Mammals
0.1	Flowers and bees
0.01	Primates
0.0002	Homo sapiens

Figure 11. The evolution on life on Earth shown in billions of years and fractions of a billion years. As the blown-up purple circle shows, our *primate* ancestors (monkeys and chimps) have been around for only about 10 million years and our own human species (called *Homo sapiens*) has been around for only a couple of hundred thousand years. Hardly any time at all on a diagram like this!

How evolution made all this happen, like a lot of things in science, is simple enough to outline but complicated in detail. The general idea is that all organisms produce more offspring than can be supported by the resources available in environments where they live. As a result, organisms compete with each other for food, water, space, mates, niches with the right temperature and whatever else they need to survive and reproduce. Those that succeed a little better in this competition reproduce a little more than the other organisms in the competing groups, and the characteristics that made them more successful therefore increase in the population. As a result of this process, called *natural selection,* the more successful organisms gradually take over until still better suited organisms come along. Eventually, the less fit organisms gradually die off (that is they become *extinct*).

Evolution by natural selection was put forward by Charles Darwin and other scientists about 150 years ago, and because it was new and seemed strange to a lot of people then, it got a lot of pushback. Today, though, evolution is understood as how all living organisms (including us) came to be. Indeed, evolution is going on right now and will continue to do so as long there is life on Earth. So we—and all other living things will continue to change in ways we can't predict, as has always been the case.

One of the bigger consequences of evolution is that brains and nervous systems came into being at some point, probably about 0. 5 to 0.6 billion years. At first, nervous systems were very simple like those that exist today in animals like the jellyfish you see washed up on the beach. Over time, however, animals evolved to have more and more complex nervous systems and eventually brains like ours.

Chapter 6

How Do Brains Develop?

Another important question is how the human brain gets to be what it is in you or me over the course of our individual lifetimes? Like many other animals, we humans start off when a sperm cell from the father fertilizes an egg cell in the mother. Almost immediately, the single fertilized egg begins to divide and soon does so at a great rate. If an egg divides to make two cells, and then the two cells divide to make four cells, and those four then divide to make eight cells, you can see that you soon get a very large number of cells. After just three or four weeks in the mother's uterus, we humans have grown into *embryos* about the size of your little finger, and most of our organs, including the brain, are recognizable. By the way, an *embryo* is what the developing baby is called at this stage when many of its parts begin take shape. After about eight weeks of development, the embryo is called a *fetus*, and finally the fetus is called a *neonate* when it is born.

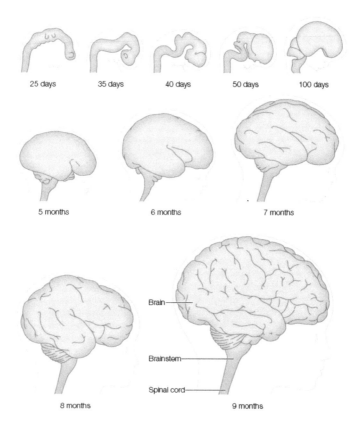

Figure 12. **The development of the human brain over the nine months before birth.**

In a human embryo the brain is first apparent as an slight enlargement at the head end of a tube of developing nerve cells, as illustrated in Figure 12. By birth our brains look more or less like they do in adults and are not all that much smaller, weighing about a kilogram. I'm sure you've noticed that baby heads are large compared to the rest of their body. The brain of a newborn contains about 100 billion nerve cells, which is about what you and I have now. Actually, you probably have a few billion more than I do, since, as I mentioned, brains shrink some with age. If you do the arithmetic and calculate how many minutes there are in nine months, it works out that on average about 250,000 nerve cells are being created *every minute* during the time before we are born!

But something in this story doesn't add up. If you have as many or more brain cells than I do, why am I writing this letter about brains to you instead of *you* telling *me* how they work? The answer may be the most important fact we know about brains: they *change* over time based on the *experiences* we have. I know a lot more than you simply because I have lived eight times longer and have had that much more experience in all the different ways you can imagine, as well as some ways you probably can't. But what is it about experience that changes in our brains as we grow up? Obviously, lots of things in bodies change over time: we get bigger, stronger, go through puberty and all the rest of what it means to mature into an adult. But what is changing our brains? It can't be the number of nerve cells since you already have just as many as I do and probably more. The answer is that *the connections between nerves cells change* based on what happens to us as we go through life. In fact, they change a whole lot.

Of course, a huge number of connections between nerve cells are already present at birth, thanks to hundreds of millions of years of brain evolution in animals that have caused the embryonic brain to develop in the way it does so that we can behave usefully once we are born. These trillions of connections can get stronger or weaker depending on what happens to us and most animals. The process of change based on experience during our lifetimes is called *neural plasticity*, which is a good name for what is going on. Something that is plastic, or has plasticity, can be shaped or molded. Think of, say, Silly Putty. But before we get into the details of plasticity, we need to talk some more about the branches coming off nerve cells and how they send information around the nervous system and why they do so. It turns out that what happens when nerve cells send information underlies the plasticity of their connections.

Chapter 7

Connections Between Nerve Cells

A good way to begin understanding how all this stuff in the brain and the rest of the nervous system actually works is what happens when someone taps your knee and your leg kicks out without your having to think about it. Figure 13 shows how sending information around the nervous system works and why it is so important. Suppose you're walking along in the woods and trip on a root. Stubbing your toe like that stretches the muscle just above your knee, which is full of sensors that are activated when this or any muscle is stretched. As shown in the diagram, these stretch sensors in the muscle send a signal to the spinal cord, where there are nerve cells that react to the signal and send a return signal back to the thigh muscle whose arrival makes it contract. As a result, your leg jerks upward. The purpose of this simple circuit—called a *reflex loop*—is to protect you: the forward movement of your leg prevents you from falling, and although you might stumble, you are spared a nasty fall. All reflex loops—and there are tons of them that do all kinds of other things in the way the nervous system influences the body—have the same general purpose: to allow you to respond quickly without having to think about what you might need to do. The result is that you have a better chance of surviving and reproducing!

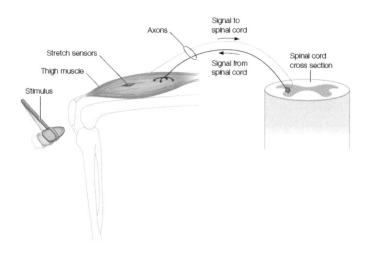

Figure 13. The knee-jerk reflex. When the knee is tapped, the thigh muscle is stretched. The stretch sensors in the muscle trigger a signal that travels up to the spinal cord. When it arrives at the spinal cord, the signal triggers a response in nerve cells that travel back to the muscle in the thigh that was stretched in the first place. The return message causes the thigh muscle to contract, making the leg "jerk."

This brings up the question of just *how* the information from the sensory receptors in your thigh muscle gets to the spinal cord, what happens when the signal arrives there, how the information returns to your thigh muscle, and, finally, what makes the muscle contract. If you look back at the picture of the nerve cell and its branches in Figure 5, you will notice that one of those branches—the *axon*—can extend a long way. In the reflex loop in Figure 13, an axon from a stretch-receptor nerve cell in the thigh muscle travels up to the spinal cord and then back down to the nerve cell in the muscle, causing the muscle contraction that causes the leg to move upward. But what makes the signal travel along the axon? And what happens at the end of the axon in the spinal cord to tell the next nerve cell in the reflex loop that it must respond? Or that tells the muscle to contract?

The answer is that axons conduct electrical impulses called *action potentials*. Very roughly speaking, something similar happens when you flip a light switch: a wire carries electricity in the circuit carries electricity to the light bulb causing it to come on. Figure 14 shows that you can record the electrical signal travelling along the axon from the spinal cord to the thigh muscle and observe the action potential as it passes by the point where it's recorded on a monitor like a TV screen. You could the same thing recording along the wire going to the light bulb, although you would much fancier equipment to do so. Looking the tick marks across the bottom of the monitor screen in Figure 14 you can see that the impulse lasts only about a thousandth of second (a millisecond) as it whisks by the recording point.

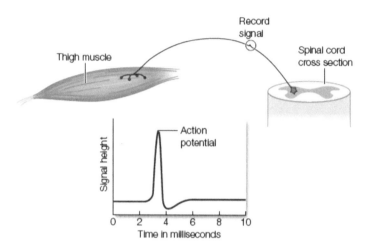

Figure 14. Axons conduct electrochemical impulses called action potentials that carry information from one place to another in the nervous system. In this example, information is carried from a nerve cell in the spinal cord to a muscle that makes the cells contract, as in Figure 13. A tiny recording probe placed in the axon can report the brief electrical signal of the action potential on a monitor screen as it goes by the probe.

But what makes the impulse travel down an axon that in you or me may be 30 or 40 centimeters long? And what about an axon running down the neck of the giraffe that may be several meters long? Although an action potential is an electrical signal that travels along an axon, it is a lot different from the electrical signal in a wire when you flip on a light. First, its speed is nothing like the speed of

41

electricity traveling along a wire. Electricity in a wire zips along at the speed of light (about 300,000 kilometers per second). The speeds of action potential impulses traveling along axons range from about 0.5 meters per second to about 100 meters per second, which is not even as fast as the speed of sound (about 340 meters per second). Why, then, do action potentials traveling along axons move so slowly? The reason is that the axon is not a wire and that the signal moving along it depends on chemistry as well as on electricity.

The best way to understand this is to imagine the burning point traveling along a length of fuse pictured in the top panel of Figure 15. You probably don't watch old cowboy movies set in the Wild West, but what I have in mind is a long fuse going from a bad guy hiding behind a rock to a stick of dynamite on a railroad track some distance away which he intends to blow up so he can rob the mail train. When he sees the train coming and lights the fuse, the burning point travels slowly along the length of the fuse—perhaps at 20 or 30 centimeters per second. The speed is slow because each little piece of the fuse must be made to burn in turn by the heat from the point just behind it. In the case of the axon, the equivalent of the burning point is the action potential signal itself, which is an electrochemical process that has much in common with the burning fuse (although the axon is not destroyed like the fuse; it recovers quickly allowing the process to be repeated may times per second). As you can see in the lower panel of Figure 15, it takes time for the action potential to travel along the axon because each point along its length has to be "set alight" to get to the next point going through the same sort of process.

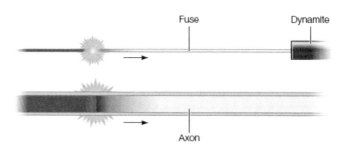

Figure 15. The fuse in a stick of dynamite as a way of understanding the relatively slow movement of action potentials along an axon. Top: The burning fuse leading to the stick of dynamite has to heat up and ignite each new piece of the fuse. Bottom: An action potential traveling along an axon behaves in much the same way: the impulse arriving at every point along the axon's length must "ignite" the next little piece making the signal travel relatively slowly.

So going on with the story about the traveling action potential, what do you think matches the explosion when the burning fuse reaches the stick of dynamite? Again, the effect is not all that different from what you see in the cowboy movie. Once the action potential reaches the end of the axon, it sets off a tiny chemical "explosion" at a special structure called a *synapse* (Figure 16). The job of the synapse is to send on the signal from the end of the axon to another nerve cell or to a target like muscle cells (see Figure 14). Here things get a little tricky but I think you'll get the general idea. As you can see in Figure 16, the end of the axon—which is very much magnified here—swells into a sort of knob that contains lots of little balls filled with a chemicals called *neurotransmitters*. The "explosion" happens when the action potential reaches the end of the axon and opens tiny

43

holes in the membrane of the knob. The holes let calcium atoms floating around outside into the knob. Once inside, the calcium causes the tiny balls filled with neurotransmitter to fuse with the membrane of the knob. Once that happens the neurotransmitter chemical in the little balls is dumped into gap between the end of the axon and the nerve cell or muscle fiber that it is in contact with.

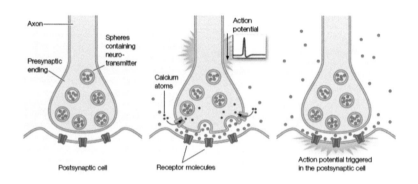

Figure 16. **Diagram of the synapse at the end of an axon showing the release of a neurotransmitter chemical onto the surface of the cell it contacts (see Figure 13).** The left panel shows the synapse at rest. The middle panel shows the arrival of the action potential, the entry of calcium atoms and the release of the neurotransmitter chemical into the gap between the pre- and postsynaptic cells. The righthand panel shows the response of the postsynaptic cell when transmitter agent molecules attach to the receptor molecules in the postsynaptic cell membrane.

Let's take a step back and make sure we are clear about the "actors" in the story diagrammed in Figure 16. Where the axon comes to an end is a meeting point, sort of like where a street meets a cross street (the cross street being the gap between the two cells that form

44

the synapse). The axon is called the *presynaptic* cell because it comes before the meeting of the two cells involved (*pre-* meaning "in front of" or "before"). And the cell to which the signal is being sent, or "transmitted," is called the *postsynaptic* cell because it comes after the meeting point (*post-* meaning "after" or "following"). I hope that makes clearer what a synapse is.

A missing piece in the synaptic transmission story so far is how the neurotransmitter chemical dumped into the gap at the end of the presynaptic axon has an effect on the next cell—that is, how does the neurotransmitter affect the postsynaptic cell on the other side of the gap? The answer is that the neurotransmitter molecules fasten onto molecules called *receptors* in the membrane of the postsynaptic cell. When the neurotransmitter attaches to the receptors, tine holes in the receptors open up let other atoms into the postsynaptic cell. The entry of these atoms sets off a new action potential in the postsynaptic cell, like "holding a match" to a new fuse (the axon) on the other side of the gap. The new action potential will now travel along the postsynaptic cell axon to wherever it happens to be going (or along the length of a muscle fiber if that is the postsynaptic cell). The result is a chain of action potentials and synapses in some part of the nervous system, such as in the knee-jerk reflex shown in Figure 13.

Chapter 8

Learning by Changing Synaptic Strength

Chapters 6 and 7 gives you pretty much all there is to understanding how information gets moved around the nervous system, whether in the brain and spinal cord or in the peripheral nervous system. Of course, the story gets a whole lot more complicated when scientists try to explain how the many different kinds of nerve cells, axons, synapses and transmitter chemicals allow our bodies to function in all the different ways they do. Keep in mind that there are many thousands of circuits in the nervous system that act more or less like the circuit underlying the knee-jerk reflex. Think, for example, of all the complicated movements you make to score a goal in soccer and all the sensory input information that is needed to do so.

That brings up the key point about synapses that I mentioned earlier : the *strength of synaptic connections can change with experience.* The strength of synaptic connections increases with practice and weakens with too little practice. For example, once you started to play soccer seriously and began to practice every day, you got better and better at it. That idea applies to pretty much everything we do. As shown in Figure 17, any of us can learn a completely unfamiliar task like "mirror writing" over just a few days. Although it may take much longer, the same goes for learning a language, how to play a musical instrument, how to stand on your head—you name it.

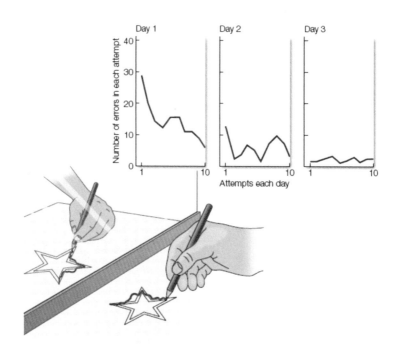

Figure 17. Mirror writing is a simple example of learning by practice. Keeping a line you are drawing inside the boundaries of the star is normally easy. But if you can only see what you are doing by looking at it in a mirror, the task becomes surprisingly hard, and at first you make lots of mistakes. As shown in the graphs, if you practice for just a few days, you can learn to do this job pretty well. Practice gradually strengthens the synaptic connections between the nerve cells that are carrying out the task of drawing the line, making you more and more able to do mirror writing successfully.

The need to learn by experience seems only natural, but what's the explanation in terms of the nerve cells and synapses? As I said, when synapses are used over and over in practicing something, they get stronger; and when they are not used, they get weaker. The ways in which this happens involve a complicated bunch of mechanisms, but I'm sure you get the idea. This ability of synapses to perform better (or worse) is the basis of *memory*, whether it is an unconscious memory like how to do mirror writing or ride a bike, or a conscious memory such as what you ate for breakfast when someone asks. These examples also make the point that how long memories last depends on their importance and how much you practice: you will remember how to shoot a soccer goal or ride a bike next month or next year, but not what you had for breakfast today unless you made an effort to do so. Either way, memories are for sure one of the most important things nervous systems give us.

Chapter 9

Why Nervous Systems Make Animals More Fit

All that raises a question we put aside earlier: why do nervous systems and brains make animals that have them more "more fit" compared to the vast majority of organisms that don't have them? I put "more fit" in quotation marks because it's not so clear which organisms really are the most successful, and you have to be careful when using phrases like that.

Over the course of the 4 billion years or so that life has existed on Earth, some pretty catastrophic things have occurred. An example you probably know about is the occasional crashing of large asteroids into the Earth. The last one of these events occurred 65 million years ago when an asteroid about 20 kilometers in diameter (the distance from Durham to Chapel Hill) hit in what is now southern Mexico, making a hole about 30 kilometers deep and 100 kilometers wide. As you might imagine, the impact left a lot of evidence. Geologists looking at what makes up the Earth's surface today—and scientists studying fossils from before and after the crash—have a good idea of how the crash affected life on Earth back then. The energy released by the impact kicked up so much dirt and dust into the atmosphere that the Earth was darkened for years. If you look at the diagram in Figure 11, you can see that 65 million years ago was the time of the dinosaurs. There were also plenty of other animals, including fish, reptiles, insects and small mammals, plus, of course, lots of plants. The darkness that covered the Earth made it much colder and caused most plants to die from lack of sunlight. Thus the plant-eating dinosaurs died out, as did the meat-eating dinosaurs, which no longer had plant eating dinosaurs or other large animals to feast on. The main survivors on land were organisms like bacteria, fungi, worms, insects and rat-like species that could live off all the debris. So who is "more fit"? Us or the organisms that survived this and even bigger catastrophes in still earlier times? It's a tricky question.

Catastrophes are related to the question of what nervous systems and brains do for us. All living things on Earth are organisms, but only some organisms are *animals*. It might seem at first that animals differ from other organisms in their size and the number of cells they have. But think again. That giant oak in your other grandfather's yard is far bigger and has more cells than any animal. In fact, animals are distinguished from other organisms mainly by having nervous systems. What, then, do animals gain by having nervous systems and brains compared with organisms that don't have them, organisms which may survive some dangers better than we would? The answer may be that nervous systems allow animals to have many more *behaviors* than organisms that don't have them. Bacteria, plants and fungi are plenty complicated and do all kinds of remarkable things, but they don't behave in ways as varied or demanding as animals, especially animals like us and other primates (monkeys, gorillas and chimps, our closest living relatives among all the animals in the world).

It should be pretty obvious that we *Homo sapiens*—even though we might not have survived a catastrophes like that huge asteroid impact—can do all kinds of things that organisms without brains can't do. Take bacteria, for example. When it comes to getting the energy they need, bacteria are limited by the nutrients (sources of energy) that happen to be nearby. Animals, on the other hand, can look around for nutrients and find them far away. Eventually some animals—such as crows and some other birds, monkeys and our closer apelike ancestors—learn to use tools. Nervous systems allow animals to do all kinds of things that organisms without nervous systems—even big complex organisms like your grandfather's oak tree—can't do.

So how do nervous systems and brains make all that happen? The answer brings us back to the synapses that connect nerve cells with each other to form associations between the different experiences we have had. For example, when you recognize your sister in a crowd you do this by associations you have made between color of her hair, appearance of her face, way she walks, the clothes she is wearing sound of her voice and so on. These associations get stored in the synaptic connections and can change throughout life; next year your sister may have different clothes and dyed her hair. If so you will store this new information by changes in connections between nerve cells being used for recognizing other people. We are also born with many associations made that everyone will need whatever their individual experience; for instance the nerve cells in the circuit that keeps us from falling down when we trip (see Figure 13). Every association among nerve cells in brains arising from synaptic connections—whether they evolved millions of years ago or were learned from experience that occurred a day earlier—helps us in some way.

If you connect one simple circuit to another, behaviors based on nerve cell connections get pretty sophisticated. For example, when you think of wanting pizza for dinner, the process is really just a more complicated version of tapping your knee. Your stomach is empty, and the axons from sensors in your gut carry that information to regions of your brain whose nerve cells produce a sense of hunger. The sense of hunger makes you think of the next meal, which makes you think of dinner, which makes you think of what might be good for dinner—and that makes you remember the taste of a good pizza. All these links are synaptic associations that are already in your brain when you of pizza for supper. More complicated to be sure, but just a bunch of nerve-cell connections that underly what we do.

It may seem weird to think that everything that is going on in your brain and the rest of your nervous system is just a bunch of simple links associated with other simple links that eventually produce very complicated behaviors that seem hard to understand. But a good rule in science is to keep things simple until you're faced with a question more complicated than can be explained by what you already know. And we know for sure that brains inherit huge numbers of associations that are already present at birth based on experience over evolutionary time, and that we make many more during our lifetimes as we learn new things.

Chapter 10

Things About the Brain We Don't Understand

Okay, given all this info, I want to end by considering one of many problems that neuroscientists are still struggling with: *how do brains make us conscious of the world*?

Right now you're aware of your surroundings, and you can therefore think and act in all the helpful ways that being conscious allows. Clearly, consciousness must somehow come from our brains, but how? Exploring this question raises some hard questions that people have been pondering for a very long time.

Let's start with the idea of a *machine* and the question of whether a machine could ever be conscious. You and I and probably everybody else thinks of a machine as a physical object made up of simple building blocks—wheels, cogs, electronic bits and so on—much like the Lego machines you like to build. All that stuff is similar to the bits and pieces that make up all kinds of complicated objects in the world we humans have made. Just like the pieces you put together to construct a model of that *Starwars* starship, the *Millennium Falcon*.

So—is the human brain, along with the rest of our nervous system, basically a machine? And if it isn't, what makes it different from a machine? As we know, the building blocks of brains and nervous systems are cells, and those cells are made up of organelles that allow them to function as they are meant to. All of these bits and pieces and their functions obey the laws of chemistry and physics. Seen that way, it would be hard to argue that brains are not machines. Sure, the cells of brains don't seem much like the plastic bricks of a Lego set, but—like Lego parts—the components of animal nervous systems are bits and pieces that are by now pretty well understood. That doesn't mean that the nervous system works like a Lego construction, but the general idea is the same. The bottom line is that it's hard to come up with any basic difference between brains and machines.

Of course, brains and nervous systems have to be stuck into bodies so that we can we can see, hear, walk around, throw a ball, etc. (Figure 18). The really puzzling question is how our machine-like brains and bodies could ever be conscious or aware of the world in the same way we are when not sleeping or under anesthesia . And I can tell you that a lot of smart people are not sure what the answer

55

is. The problem is that if there is no basic difference between the components that make animals work and the components that make machines work, then it is hard to argue that machines we might make in the future could not eventually be aware, just as we are. That doesn't mean that computer-driven robots are going to be conscious any time soon. But it's logical enough to suppose that the machines we call computers and robots will someday have a sense of awareness, just as we do.

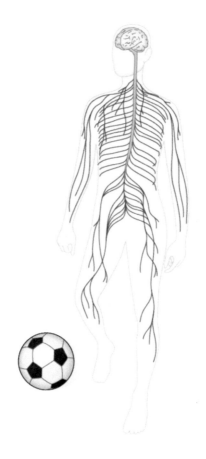

Figure 18. Brains need bodies to create actions and other behaviors that make the things we want to happen in the world take place.

Of course, many people don't want to accept this idea. It makes us seem no better than the robots and computers, which is scary. Who wants to think of themselves as a Roomba vacuum cleaner? But by the time robots and computer-like brains become as sophisticated as we are (or even smarter), we should welcome their arrival. And getting there has already begun. You may beat me at chess but computers that learn how to play by changing their connections can now easily beat the best human players at chess or any other game, including video games like Minecraft and Starcraft. And that is just the beginning.

If you look around the world today, it is clear that we human beings are nothing to brag about and that we could do a whole lot better in pretty much everything we aim to do. I will not live long enough to see how all this begins to play out in conscious machines whose "brains" can go further than we have, but you very well might.

* * *

Of course, I could be wrong. But IMHO opinion, science—looking at the evidence— is the best way to sort out what are brains are, where they are now heading, and how we can help ours or others get there.

Mini-Dictionary

animals Complex organisms that are distinguished by having nervous systems.

association A link between made in the brain by synaptic connections.

autonomic nervous system The part of the nervous system the controls the smooth muscles in the body's organs.

autopsy Examination of a dead body to determine or confirm the cause of death.

axon A branch coming off the nerve cell body that carries information to another nerve cell or other target cell often over long distances.

bacteria (s. bacterium) Single-cell organisms that lack a nucleus; examples are the germs in your gut, on your skin and pretty much everywhere else in the world.

behavior The output of the nervous system, which can be a motor action, a sensation, a perception, an emotion, a focus of attention or a thought.

biopsy The piece of tissue that a surgeon removes from a patient to see what the problem is—for example, whether the piece of tissue shows evidence of cancer.

brainstem The component of the brain that connects the cerebral hemispheres and the cerebellum to the spinal cord.

cell body The part of any cell that contains the nucleus and other organelles; the axon and dendrite branches extend from the nerve cell body.

centimeter A hundredth part of a meter, which is a little less than half an inch.

central nervous system The brain and spinal cord.

cerebrum (pl. cerebra) The two cerebral hemispheres taken together.

cerebellum A part of the brain tucked beneath the occipital lobes at the back of the cerebral hemispheres. Mainly responsible for monitoring and correcting errors of movement.

erebral hemispheres The two halves of the cerebrum.

consciousness Awareness of ourselves and the world around us.

dendrites The branches coming off nerve cell bodies that receive synaptic inputs from other nerve cells.

electron microscope A microscope that uses electrons to magnify objects at high power than light.

embryo The developing baby in the uterus between about the second to the eighth week of development.

evolution The gradual change of organisms since life on Earth began that has given rise to all living things today. See *natural selection.*

fetus The developing baby in the uterus after eight weeks of gestation.

genes The stretches of DNA in cell nuclei that code for the construction proteins and other biologically important molecules.

geologists Scientists who study the structure and composition of the Earth, particularly its surface layers.

heart muscle The special muscle type that allows the heart to contract on a continual basis.

hemoglobin The protein molecule in red blood cells that carries oxygen to the body tissues and removes CO_2.

hominin The name given to our human ancestors from the evolution of great apes to the appearance *Homo sapiens*, the modern human species.

Homo sapiens The species name given to modern humans.

information A meaningful signal that can be distinguished from a noisy background.

light microscope A microscope that uses light waves to magnify objects; their magnification is limited by the wavelengths of light.

lobes The four large components of each cerebral hemisphere identified by looking at the brain surface.

meter A measure of distance that forms the basic unit of the metric system; about three and a half inches more than a yard in the English system.

metric system A worldwide measuring system based on the meter.

microscopic Not visible to the naked eye.

micron (or *micrometer*) A thousandth part of a millimeter.

millimeter A thousandth part of a meter.

molecules Combinations of atoms that are held together as a functional unit in chemistry.

anometer A billionth part of the meter.

natural selection The evolutionary process that lets the organisms best suited to their environment survive while organisms that are less fit die off.

nerve cell One the billions of cells that make up the nervous system; characterized by an axon and dendritic branches.

nerve fiber A synonym for the axon that comes off a nerve cell body.

nervous system All parts of the central and peripheral nervous systems.

neuron A synonym for nerve cell.

neuropathologists Medical doctors who specialize in identifying diseases of the brain based on anatomy and chemistry.

organisms All living things.

organs Large collections of cells that have come together as visible structures to serve a particular function; examples are the eyes, the heart, the lungs and the stomach.

paleontologists Scientists who study the history of life on Earth by examining fossils.

pathologists Medical doctors who specialize in diagnosing diseases by looking at autopsy specimens or at tissue removed from patients during surgery.

peripheral nerves Bundles of nerve axons that extend from the brainstem and spinal cord to supply targets in the rest of the body with nerves.

peripheral nervous system The nervous system excluding the central nervous system.

photons Particles that carry light energy as waves.

picometer A trillionth part of a meter.

postsynaptic cell A nerve or muscle cell that receives a synaptic ending from a presynaptic axon.

presynaptic terminal The ending of a nerve cell axon that releases a neurotransmitter chemical onto a postsynaptic cell.

primate A class of animals that includes monkeys, great apes and humans.

protein Molecules made up of long chains of subunits called amino acids.

receptors Molecules in a membrane's postsynaptic nerve or muscle cells that respond to neurotransmitter molecules released by presynaptic terminals.

reflex A simple loop between sensory input in some behavioral output.

sections Slices of chemically treated tissues that can be looked at with a microscope.

sense organs Organs such as the eye and ear that evolved to take in sensory information from the environment.

sensory information Stimuli from the environment that sense organs can respond to.

skeletal muscles Muscles attached to the bones of the skeleton that allow us to move.

smooth muscle A special class of muscle that generates movement in organs such as those that push food along in the gut.

species A classification of animals based on their ability to interbreed; dogs and cats are different species because they cannot breed with each other

stimulus (pl. stimuli) Energy from the environment (or from inside us) that sense organs respond to.

synapse A junction between nerve cells (or nerve cells and muscle cells) that transmits information by means of neurotransmitter chemicals.

uterus The reproductive organ in a woman's pelvis in which fertilized eggs develop into babies.

ventricles Spaces filled with a salty fluid that circulates throughout the brain and helps maintain its chemical balance.

wavelengths The distance in meters or fractions of meters between one wave peak and the next; they are measured in waterways, light, sound, and other wave phenomena.

Conversion Table of Metric to English Measurements

1 centimeter = 0.4 inches

1 meter = 3.3 feet or 1.1 yards

1 kilometer = 0.6 miles

1 kilogram = 2.2 pounds

Acknowledgements

I am especially grateful to Paul Betz for suggesting this book; to Paul Betz, Will Burns, Sara Ross Burns, Shannon Ravenel and Wyndham Robertson for corrections on the manuscript; and to Jan Troutt for the illustrations.